In Your Pocket:
The DMCA

Limit of Liability: While the author has used her best efforts in preparing the book, she makes no representations with respect to accuracy or completeness of the content. The content contained herein may not be relevant to your situation. Consult with a professional where applicable. The author shall not be liable for any commercial damage, including but not limited to special, incidental, consequential, or other damages.

ISBN - 978-0-557-13781-7

PREFACE

The following chapters offer brief descriptions of the different sections of the DMCA. This does not cover all of the sections in detail, but is a brief overview of the different sections of the DMCA.

Keep in mind that the text is a summary of the actual law. If you find anything that you believe is incorrect or misrepresented, please contact the author about these points. This is in no way to be construed as letter of the law. The author is not a lawyer, but a technical communicator attempting to take the law and make this law easier to read and understand. Some of the words in the definitions and summaries are actual text, taken from the DMCA.

The following section summaries were originally intended to be a portion of the book, "A Decade of the DMCA".

Each section of the DMCA is addressed in this pocket book.

These sections of the DMCA with summaries are solely the author's summary based on research into the DMCA over the past 10 years.
These summaries were very useful to the author while researching numerous DMCA cases and issues. The book can be used as a

quick reference. Further research into the law to verify the validity is suggested.

Remember that the author is not a lawyer and nothing in this book is to be considered advice. If you need legal advice, please consult a lawyer.

The following is from the final joint version of the DMCA

SECTION 1. SHORT TITLE.

This Act may be cited as the `Digital Millennium Copyright Act'.

SEC. 2. TABLE OF CONTENTS.

TITLE I--WIPO TREATIES IMPLEMENTATION

TITLE II--ONLINE COPYRIGHT INFRINGEMENT LIABILITY LIMITATION

TITLE III--COMPUTER MAINTENANCE OR REPAIR COPYRIGHT EXEMPTION

TITLE IV--MISCELLANEOUS PROVISIONS

TITLE V--PROTECTION OF CERTAIN ORIGINAL DESIGNS

Sec. 505. Effective date.

TITLE I--WIPO TREATIES IMPLEMENTATION

SEC. 101. SHORT TITLE.

This title may be cited as the `WIPO Copyright and Performances and Phonograms Treaties Implementation Act of 1998'

TITLE I – SEC. 101 and 102

These sections are the short title and technical amendments.

TITLE I - 103. COPYRIGHT PROTECTION SYSTEMS
AND
COPYRIGHT MANAGEMENT INFORMATION

Chapter 12 was added to Title 17 as Copyright Protection and Management Systems. This chapter includes:

1201. Circumvention of copyright protection systems.

1202. Integrity of copyright management information.

1203. Civil remedies.

1204. Criminal offenses and penalties.

1205. Savings clause.

Circumvention of copyright protection systems

1201 a (1)

Summary

This section states that no one can circumvent a technological measure that effectively controls access to a work protected under this title.

What would qualify as a technological measure that controls access to a work?

Wellington Grey distributes a presentation online done around 2005. This presentation compares analog and digital technological measures. Mr. Grey went on a road trip and the GPS software required agreeing to a license by breaking of a seal on the CD. However, the license was on the CD. Mr. Grey bypassed this seal by opening the envelope, using scissors along the bottom of the CD case. This is an interesting presentation of analog applications of the DMCA and can be found at:

http://www.slideshare.net/wellington_grey/the-digital-millennium-copyright-act-in-the-real-world-presentation

From the Adobe case against Sklyarov (Elcomsoft), we learned that even rot13 can be considered a technological measure that effectively controls access to a work. Even a weak encryption scheme (one that a child can comprehend) qualifies as an effective measure to control access.

This took effect 2 years after the DMCA was enacted.

2 years after 1998 = 2000.

Sec. 1201 a (2)

Summary

No one can

- manufacture
- import
- offer to the public
- provide
- traffic

in any

- technology
- product
- service
- device

or

- component or part thereof

is primarily designed or produced for the purpose of circumventing a technological measure that effectively controls access to a work protected under the title; or

has only limited commercially significant purpose or use other than to circumvent a technological measure that effectively controls access to a work protected under this title

or

is marketed by that person or another acting in concert with that person with that person's knowledge for use in circumventing a technological measure that effectively controls access to a work protected under this title.

1201 a (3)

Definitions

Circumvent a Technological Measure

- To descramble
- To decrypt
- To bypass, avoid, remove, deactivate or impair a technology without the permission of the copyright owner

Technological Measure

Measure that "effectively controls access to a work"

if the measure, in the ordinary course of its operation, requires:

- the application of information
- a process
- a treatment

with the authority of the copyright owner, to gain access to the work.

Additional Violations
1201 (b)

Summary

(1) Similar to 1201(a)(2), 1201(b)**(1)** uses similar text to protect
the copyright owner.

No one can

- manufacture
- import
- offer to the public
- provide
- traffic

in any

- technology
- product
- service
- device

or

- component or part thereof

that is primarily designed or produced for the purpose of
circumventing protection afforded by a technological measure
that effectively protects a right of a copyright owner under this
title in a work or a portion thereof;

or

has only limited commercially significant purpose or use other than to circumvent protection afforded by a technological measure that effectively protects a right of a copyright owner under this title in a work or a portion thereof;

or

is marketed by that person or another acting in concert with that person with that person's knowledge for use in circumventing protection afforded by a technological measure that effectively protects a right of a copyright owner under this title in a work or a portion thereof.

1201 b (2)
Definitions

Circumvent protection afforded by a technological measure:
avoiding, bypassing, removing, deactivating, or otherwise
impairing a technological measure; and

**Technological measure "effectively protects a right of a
copyright owner under this title"**
if the measure, in the ordinary course of its operation, prevents,
restricts, or otherwise limits the exercise of a right of a copyright
owner under this title.

Other Rights, Etc., Not Affected
1201 (c)

Summary

(1) Nothing in this section should affect rights or defenses to infringement, including fair use.

(2) The next section 1201 (c) (2) covers respondeat superior and contributory liability, stating that nothing in this section shall enlarge or diminish these liabilities for infringement in connection with any technology, product, service, device, component, or part thereof.

(3) Nothing in this section regards that nothing in this section requires the design as long as the product or component or part is integrated and does not fall within the prohibitions in (a)(2) or (b)(1).

(4) Finally, free speech or the press is included. Nothing in this section shall enlarge or diminish any rights of free speech or the press for activities using electronics, telecommunications, or computing products.

Exemptions for Libraries, Archives, and Educational Institutions
1201 (d)

Summary

If a nonprofit library, archive or educational institution gets access to a copyrighted work that has been commercially exploited, with the only intention as to make a good faith decision as to whether to get a copy of the work for the purpose of "engaging in conduct permitted under this title", or perhaps, legally using a copyright work, the library, archive or educational institution will **NOT** be found in violation of circumvention of technological measures that effectively controls access to a work protected.

What does this mean? Well, this could mean that a nonprofit library, archive or educational institution have exemptions from violations.

Does this mean a library can use a commercially available program to decrypt the access to a work in order to determine whether to purchase that work as long as they don't keep the program for any time longer than is necessary to base their decision and don't use the program for any other purpose? This seems to be the case. Of course, it seems that the exemption only applies when an identical copy of that work is not "reasonably" available in some other form.

The nonprofit library, archives, or educational institution that intentionally violates uses this clause for commercial advantage or financial gain will be subject to civil remedies for a first offense under 1203.

Reference 1203

- and for additional offenses will be subject to 1203 and no longer be eligible for the exemption.
- Libraries, archives and educational institutions can NOT "manufacture, import, offer this program to the public, or otherwise traffic in any technology, product, service, component, or part thereof, which circumvents a technological measure" but it seems they can use one.
- A library or archive must be open to the public or available to researchers within and from the outside of the library or archive.

In October 2003, 4 exemptions were approved. One of these exemptions assisted in archiving of vintage software.

The TEACH Act of 2002 includes online education standards.

Reference Title 17 Section 110(2)(D)(ii)(II)

This law also includes a section on interfering with regard to obstructing encryption.

II) does not engage in conduct that could reasonably be expected to interfere with technological measures used by copyright owners to prevent such retention or unauthorized further dissemination;

In other words, does not engage in digital transmission, the transmission does not obstruct technological measures put into place by copyright owners to prevent unauthorized use. These may include watermarks, encryption or DRM.

Law Enforcement, Intelligence, and other
Government Activities
1201 (e)

Summary

Legally authorized government agencies and employees, including employees or agents of a State, the United States, or "political subdivision" of a State, including someone on contract for either of these parties is not prohibited from circumventing a technological measures in the course of their authorized "investigative, protective, information security or intelligence activity".

What are some examples of government use?

Perhaps, a state trooper needs to circumvent a technological measure of a computer that was confiscated. The authorities need to circumvent this measure in order to obtain evidence of a crime.

Reverse Engineering
1201 (f)

Summary

You may circumvent a technological measure that "effectively" controls access to a particular portion of a program for the sole purpose of identifying and analyzing the elements that are necessary for interoperability of an independently created program as long as this has not been readily available to the person engaging in circumvention, as long as the identification and analysis do not constitute infringement.

The information acquired through the acts may be made available to others if the person provides information for the sole purpose of enabling interoperability of an independently created computer program with other programs and to the extent that this does not constitute infringement or violate laws.

Definition: Interoperability

The ability to computer programs to exchange information, and of such programs mutually to use the information which has been exchanged.

Encryption Research

1201 (g)

Summary

Encryption research is permitted under this act. However, the law states that in spite of the the provisions of subsection (a)(1)(A) (circumvention of a technological measure), it is not a violation when a person circumvents a technological measure with regard to a copy, phonorecord, performance, or display of a published work in the course of an act of good faith encryption research.

Permissible acts of encryption research
1201 (g)(2)

The person must meet the following requirements:

A. Lawfully obtain an encrypted copy, phonorecord, performance, or display of the published work

B. The act must be necessary to conduct such encryption research;

C. The person must have made a good faith effort to obtain authorization before the circumvention.

   and

D. If the act does not constitute infringement under this title or a violation of applicable law other than this section, including section 1030 of title 18 and those provisions of title 18 amended by the Computer Fraud and Abuse Act of 1986.

FACTORS IN DETERMINING EXEMPTION
1201 (g)(3)

To establish if someone qualifies for the encryption research exemption, the following is considered:

A. Was the information obtained from encryption research? If so, was the information disseminated "in a manner reasonably calculated to advance the state of knowledge or development of encryption technology" rather than to facilitate infringement of this title or other laws in general, including privacy and security law.

B. Was the person legitimately studying, was employed by or trained and experienced in encryption technology?

C. Did the person provide the copyright owner of the work a notice of the findings including documentation of the research and does the person have the timeline of when the notice was provided?

1201 (g)(2)
DEFINITIONS

Encryption Research : Activities necessary to identify and analyze flaws and vulnerabilities of encryption technologies applied to copyrighted works, if these activities are conducted to advance the state of knowledge in the field of encryption technology or to assist in the development of encryption products

Encryption Technology: The scrambling and descrambling of information using mathematical formulas or algorithms.

1201(g)(4)

Summary

Not a violation to develop and employ a means for circumventing a technological measure for the purpose of performing acts of good faith encryption research and provide the technological means to another person with whom he/she is working collaboratively for the purpose of conducting acts of good faith encryption research or for the purpose of having the other person validate his/her acts of good faith encryption research.

Report to Congress
1201(g)(5)

The Register of Copyrights and the Assistant Secretary for Communications and Information of the Department of Commerce shall jointly report to the Congress on the effect this subsection has had on encryption research and the development of encryption technology. The report is to include the following:

- the adequacy and effectiveness of technological measures designed to protect copyrighted works; and
- protection of copyright owners against the unauthorized access to their encrypted copyrighted works.
- The report shall include legislative recommendations, if any.

MINORS
1201 (h)

Summary

This section indicates a consideration of the intent of 1201a with regards to preventing access of minors to material.

Legal References

`(h) EXCEPTIONS REGARDING MINORS- In applying subsection (a) to a component or part, the court may consider the necessity for its intended and actual incorporation in a technology, product, service, or device, which--

    `(1) does not itself violate the provisions of this title; and

    `(2) has the sole purpose to prevent the access of minors to material on the Internet.

Protection of Personally Identifying Information
1201 (i)

Summary

It is not a violation to circumvent a technological measure if the measure contains the capability of collecting personal information. One question that can be raised here is: what kind of personal information?

Section A

This section allows bypassing encryption to prevent

"information reflecting the online activities of a natural person who seeks to gain access to the work protected;"

This section does not apply to "a technological measure, or a work it protects, that does not collect or disseminate personally identifying information and that is disclosed to a user as not having or using such capability."

Security Testing

1201 (j)

Summary

In this section, there are several permitted acts or exemptions for security testing.

The factors in consideration include whether the information was used for the sole purpose of promoting the security of the computer, computer network, user of the computer, and whether the information obtained from the testing was used in a manner that does not facilitate infringement. This also includes as long as it is not a violation of privacy or breach of security.

Furthermore, it is not a violation of 1201 (a) (2) to develop, produce, distribute, or employ technical means for the sole purpose of security testing as long as the technology does not violate (a) (2).

This section specifically offers protection from 1201(a)(2), so long as the item is not primarily designed or produced for the purpose of circumventing a technological measure that effectively controls access to a work protected under the title. In other words, this is explicit protection for security testing and actually seems to promote the security of computers, networks, and the user. If you meet the factors for this section, then no violation. However, this section includes this text:

> **and whether the information obtained from the testing was used in a manner that does not facilitate**

infringement

This is potentially the disadvantage. In this case, the verbiage seems a bit ambiguous and could lend to simply allowing security testing if permission is sought by the owner or if the owner employs an individual to conduct security testing. The TEACH Act, while it includes what can be done with regard to online education, does not address this section.

Analog devices and technological measures
1201 (k)

Summary

Certain Analog Devices and Certain Technological Measures 18 months after the DMCA was enacted, no person could provide, manufacture, import, etc.

- ➢ **VHS recorders**
- ➢ **8mm format analog video cassette recorder**
- ➢ **Beta format analog video cassette recorder**
  Does not apply until there are 1000 sold in the US in any one year (following enactment, of course).
- ➢ **8mm format analog video cassette recorder** that is not a camcorder. Does not apply until 20,000 recorders sold in any one year after enactment.
- ➢ **Analog Video Cassette Recorder** that uses NTSC format input and is not covered in the first 4 items above.

If the recorder complied to the gain control copy control technology, then it is not a violation. However, if the recorder did not have the gain control copy control and was manufactured, imported or distributed, the person performing the distribution or manufacture would be in violation of the DMCA.

For companies that were not already manufacturers of recorders, they would need to conform to the 4 line colorstripe copy control initially and thereafter.

Encoding Restrictions
1201 (k) (2)

Summary

This section covers restrictions on applying the automatic gain control copy control technology or colorstripe copy control technology to prevent or limit consumer copying.

There are some exceptions.

A. a single transmission, or specified group of transmissions, of live events or of audiovisual works for which a member of the public has exercised choice in selecting the transmissions, including the content of the transmissions or the time of receipt of such transmissions, or both, and as to which such member is charged a separate fee for each such transmission or specified group of transmissions;

B. from a copy of a transmission of a live event or an audiovisual work if such transmission is provided by a channel or service where payment is made by a member of the public for such channel or service in the form of a subscription fee that entitles the member of the public to receive all of the programming contained in such channel or service;

C. from a physical medium containing one or more prerecorded audiovisual works; or

D. from a copy of a transmission described in subparagraph (A) or from a copy made from a physical medium described in subparagraph (C).

In the event that a transmission meets both the conditions set forth in subparagraph (A) and those set forth in subparagraph (B), the transmission shall be treated as a transmission described in subparagraph (A).

INAPPLICABILITY
1201 (k) (3)

Now that you have pondered calling the police and a defense for the yard sale owner, this section clarifies several areas where the above is not applicable.

A. does not require any analog video cassette camcorder to conform to the automatic gain control copy control technology with respect to any video signal received through a camera lens;

B. does not apply to the manufacture, importation, offer for sale, provision of, or other trafficking in, any professional analog video cassette recorder; or

C. apply to the offer for sale or provision of, or other trafficking in, any previously owned analog video cassette recorder, if such recorder was legally manufactured and sold when new and not subsequently modified in violation of paragraph (1)(B).

1201 (k) (4)

DEFINITIONS

A. **Analog video cassette recorder**

Device that records, or a device that includes a function that records, on electromagnetic tape in an analog format the electronic impulses produced by the video and audio portions of a television program, motion picture, or other form of audiovisual work.

B. **Analog video cassette camcorder** means an analog video cassette recorder that contains a recording function that operates through a camera lens and through a video input that may be connected with a television or other video playback device.

C. **An analog video cassette recorder conforms** to the automatic gain control copy control technology if it--

(i)   detects one or more of the elements of such technology and does not record the motion picture or transmission protected by such technology;

or

(ii) records a signal that, when played back, exhibits a meaningfully distorted or degraded display.

D. **Professional analog video cassette recorder** An analog video cassette recorder that is designed, manufactured, marketed, and intended for use by a person who regularly employs such a device for a lawful business or industrial use, including making, performing, displaying, distributing, or transmitting copies of motion pictures on a commercial scale.

E. **VHS format', `8mm format', `Beta format', `automatic gain control copy control technology', `colorstripe copy control technology', `four-line version of the colorstripe copy control technology', and `NTSC'** have the meanings that are commonly understood in the consumer electronics and motion picture industries as of the date of the enactment of this chapter.

VIOLATIONS
1201 (k) (5)

Any violation of paragraph (1) of this subsection shall be treated as a violation of subsection (b)(1) of this section. Any violation of paragraph (2) of this subsection shall be deemed an `act of circumvention' for the purposes of section 1203(c)(3)(A) of this chapter.

Integrity of copyright management information
FALSE COPYRIGHT MANAGEMENT INFORMATION
1202 (a)

Summary

This section covers knowingly and intentionally concealing or facilitating infringement.

1. No providing false copyright management information
2. No distribution or import for distribution false copyright management information.

REMOVAL OR ALTERATION OF COPYRIGHT
MANAGEMENT INFORMATION
1202 (b)

Unless you have the authorization of the copyright owner or the law, you may not

1. intentionally remove or alter any copyright management information
2. distribute or import for distribution copyright management information knowing that the copyright management information has been removed or altered without authority of the copyright owner or the law
3. distribute, import for distribution, or publicly perform works, copies of works, or phonorecords, knowing that copyright management information has been removed or altered without authority of the copyright owner or the law

"knowing, or, with respect to civil remedies under section 1203, having reasonable grounds to know, that it will induce, enable, facilitate, or conceal an infringement of any right under this title."

1202 (c)

Definitions

Copyright Management Information

means any of the following information conveyed in connection
with copies or phonorecords of a work or performances or displays
of a work, including in digital form, except that such term does not
include any personally identifying information about a user of a
work or of a copy, phonorecord, performance, or display of a
work:

1. The title and other information identifying the work, including
    the information set forth on a notice of copyright.
2. The name of, and other identifying information about, the
    author of a work.
3. The name of, and other identifying information about, the
    copyright owner of the work, including the information set
    forth in a notice of copyright.
4. With the exception of public performances of works by radio
    and television broadcast stations, the name of, and other
    identifying information about, a performer whose performance
    is fixed in a work other than an audiovisual work.
5. With the exception of public performances of works by radio
    and television broadcast stations, in the case of an audiovisual
    work, the name of, and other identifying information about, a
    writer, performer, or director who is credited in the audiovisual

work.

6. Terms and conditions for use of the work.

7. Identifying numbers or symbols referring to such information or links to such information.

8. Such other information as the Register of Copyrights may prescribe by regulation, except that the Register of Copyrights may not require the provision of any information concerning the user of a copyrighted work.

LAW ENFORCEMENT, INTELLIGENCE, AND OTHER GOVERNMENT ACTIVITIES

1202 (d)

Summary

This section covers any lawfully authorized investigative, protective, information security, or intelligence activity of an officer, agent, or employee of the United States, a State, or a political subdivision of a State, or a person acting pursuant to a contract with the United States, a State, or a political subdivision of a State.

Definition

Information Security

Activities carried out in order to identify and address the vulnerabilities of a government computer, computer system, or computer network.

LIMITATIONS ON LIABILITY
1202 (e)

Summary

The following section sets limitations on the liability for cable and broadcast where there is no intent to conceal infringement.

1. ANALOG TRANSMISSIONS

There is no liability for broadcast or cable transmission if:

A. avoiding the activity that constitutes such violation is not technically feasible or would create an undue financial hardship on such person; and

B. such person did not intend, by engaging in such activity, to induce, enable, facilitate, or conceal infringement of a right under this title.

2. DIGITAL TRANSMISSIONS

A. If a digital transmission standard for the placement of copyright management information for a category of works is set in a voluntary, consensus standard-setting process involving a representative cross-section of broadcast stations or cable systems and copyright owners of a category of works that are intended for public performance by such stations or systems, a person identified in paragraph (1) shall not be liable for a violation of subsection (b) with respect to the particular copyright management information addressed by such standard if—

i the placement of such information by someone other than such person is not in accordance with such standard; and

ii the activity that constitutes such violation is not intended to induce, enable, facilitate, or conceal infringement of a right under this title.

Legal Reference

`(B) Until a digital transmission standard has been set pursuant to subparagraph (A) with respect to the placement of copyright management information for a category or works, a person identified in paragraph (1) shall not be liable for a violation of subsection (b) with respect to such copyright management information, if the activity that constitutes such violation is not intended to induce, enable, facilitate, or conceal infringement of a right under this title, and if--

`(i) the transmission of such information by such person would result in a perceptible visual or aural degradation of the digital signal; or

`(ii) the transmission of such information by such person would conflict with--

`(I) an applicable government regulation relating to transmission of information in a digital signal;

`(II) an applicable industry-wide standard relating to the transmission of information in a digital signal that was adopted by a voluntary consensus standards body prior to the effective date of this chapter; or

`(III) an applicable industry-wide standard relating to the transmission of information in a digital signal that was adopted in a voluntary, consensus standards-setting process open to participation by a representative cross-section of broadcast stations or cable systems and copyright owners of a category of works that are intended for public performance by such stations or systems.

`(3) DEFINITIONS- As used in this subsection--

`(A) the term `broadcast station' has the meaning given that term in section 3 of the Communications Act of 1934 (47 U.S.C. 153); and

`(B) the term `cable system' has the meaning given that term in section 602 of the Communications Act of 1934 (47 U.S.C. 522).

Civil remedies
1203.

Summary

The following section discusses the civil remedies for the "injured" based on a violation of 1201 or 1202.

Civil Actions
1203 (a)

If someone is injured by a violation of 1201 or 1201, this person my bring a civil action in an "appropriate US district court".

POWERS OF THE COURT
1203 (b)

In a civil action, the court:

1. May grant temporary and permanent injunctions to prevent further violation

   Note: The court shall NOT impose a prior restraint on free speech or the press as these are protected under the 1st amendment.

2. May order impounding devices or products that is in "the custody or control of the alleged violator and that the court has reasonable cause to believe was involved in a violation"

3. May award damages

4. At the court's discretion, may allow the recovery of costs by or against any party other than the United States or an officer thereof

5. May award reasonable attorney's fees to the prevailing party

6. May, upon finding a violation, order the remedial modification or the destruction of any device or product involved in the violation that is in the custody or control of the violator or has been impounded under paragraph (2) as part of the final judgment or decree.

AWARD OF DAMAGES
1203 (c)

1. General

    A violation carries with it the following:

    A. the actual damages and any additional profits of the violator, as provided in paragraph (2), or
    B. statutory damages, as provided in paragraph (3).

2. ACTUAL DAMAGES

    The court shall award to the complaining party the actual damages suffered by the party as a result of the violation, and any profits of the violator that are attributable to the violation and are not taken into account in computing the actual damages, if the complaining party elects such damages at any time before final judgment is entered.

3. STATUTORY DAMAGES

    A. At any time before final judgment is entered, a complaining party may elect to recover an award of statutory damages for each violation of section 1201 in the sum of not less than $200 or more than $2,500 per act of circumvention, device, product, component, offer, or performance of service, as the court considers just.
    B. At any time before final judgment is entered, a complaining

party may elect to recover an award of statutory damages for each violation of section 1202 in the sum of not less than $2,500 or more than $25,000.

4. REPEATED VIOLATIONS

In any case in which the injured party sustains the burden of proving, and the court finds, that a person has violated section 1201 or 1202 within 3 years after a final judgment was entered against the person for another such violation, the court may increase the award of damages up to triple the amount that would otherwise be awarded, as the court considers just.

5. Innocent violations

A. IN GENERAL

The court in its discretion may reduce or remit the total award of damages in any case in which the violator sustains the burden of proving, and the court finds, that the violator was not aware and had no reason to believe that its acts constituted a violation.

B. NONPROFIT LIBRARY, ARCHIVES, OR EDUCATIONAL INSTITUTIONS

In the case of a nonprofit library, archives, or educational institution, the court shall remit damages in any case in which the library, archives, or educational institution sustains the burden of proving, and the court finds, that the library, archives, or educational institution was not aware and had no reason to believe that its acts constituted a violation.

Criminal offenses and penalties

1204

Summary

Any person that violates section 1201 or 1202 intentionally and for commercial benefit or financial gain will be, for the first offense:

fined not more than 500,000

or

imprisoned for not more than 5 years or both.

For any subsequent offense the person shall be fined not more than 1,000,000 or imprisoned more than 10 years or both.

LIMITATION FOR NONPROFIT LIBRARY, ARCHIVES, OR EDUCATIONAL INSTITUTION

1204 (b)

Section (a) does not apply to nonprofit libraries, archives, or educational institutions.

STATUTE OF LIMITATIONS

1204 (c)

Proceedings must be commenced within 5 years after the cause of action arose.

Savings clause

1205

Summary

Legal References

'Nothing in this chapter abrogates, diminishes, or weakens the provisions of, nor provides any defense or element of mitigation in a criminal prosecution or civil action under, any Federal or State law that prevents the violation of the privacy of an individual in connection with the individual's use of the Internet.'.

1204 (b) CONFORMING AMENDMENT- The table of chapters for title 17, United States Code, is amended by adding after the item relating to chapter 11 the following:

1201'.

Treaties - Section 103

The World Intellectual Property Organization (WIPO) Copyright
Treaty and the WIPO Performances and Phonograms Treaty can be
found at the December 20, 1996 Diplomatic Conference on Certain
Copyright and Neighboring Rights Questions
http://www.wipo.org/eng/diplconf/distrib/94dc.htm

Copyright laws in many countries were amended in order to adhere
to the adopted treaty.

Article 11

Obligations concerning Technological Measures

Contracting Parties shall provide adequate legal protection and effective legal remedies against the circumvention of effective technological measures that are used by authors in connection with the exercise of their rights under this Treaty or the Berne Convention and that restrict acts, in respect of their works, which are not authorized by the authors concerned or permitted by law.

Chapter12 of the DMCA was added to adhere to this section. However many people believe the DMCA goes a little further than what was required.

There is a timeline regarding the DMCA legislation.
http://www.arl.org/info/frn/copy/primer.html#part1

Libraries believed they would get exemptions. Here is a link explaining what really happened.

http://www.arl.org/info/frn/copy/pr110100.html
http://www.arl.org/info/frn/copy/pr110100.html
http://www.wto.org/english/tratop_e/trips_e/intel3_e.htm
http://www.wto.org/english/tratop_e/trips_e/intel3_e.htm
http://www.wto.org/english/tratop_e/trips_e/intel3_e.htm

TITLE II--ONLINE COPYRIGHT INFRINGEMENT LIABILITY LIMITATION

TITLE II--ONLINE COPYRIGHT INFRINGEMENT LIABILITY LIMITATION

Summary

Title II or the online service provider liability section outlines the limitations of liability to the ISP with regards to copyright violations.

What is ISP Safe Harbor?

Basically, service providers are not liable where the following criteria are met:

- Provider has no actual knowledge that the material on the network or system was infringing
- If the provider does know the material is on the system or network, the provider is not aware that infringing activity is present
- The provider acts quickly to remove or disable infringing materials
- The provider does not financially gain, directly, from the infringing activity
- The provider responds quickly to remove material once notified.

SYSTEM CACHING

512 (b)

Summary

The service provider is not liable for cache of infringing materials.
This applies to automatic storage. Once a notification is received,
the ISP must stop caching any infringing material (Chilling, 2008).

The service provider is not liable for material that is:

1. made available online by a person other than the service
    provider;
2. transmitted from the person described other than the service
    provider, through the network, to a person other than the
    person who is making content available who is not the
    service provider, at the direction of that other person; and
3. the storage is processed using an automatic technical
    process for the purpose of making the material available to
    users of the system or network who, after the material is
    transmitted through the network as described above,
    request access to the material from the person who made
    the content available that is not the service provider.

If the following conditions are met:

*   The material described in paragraph is transmitted to the users
    without modification to its content from the manner in which

the material was transmitted from the person who is not the provider and who is making content available;

- The service provider described complies with rules concerning refreshing, reloading, or other updating of the material when specified by the person making the material available online in accordance with a generally accepted industry standard data communications protocol for the system or network through which that person makes the material available, except that this subparagraph applies only if those rules are not used by the person making the content available who is not the service provider, to prevent or unreasonably impair the intermediate storage to which this subsection applies.

ISP SAFE HARBOR

Examples of Use

There are many cases where Google received notifications with regards to their cache option. While they are not a service provider, but a location tool, the provisions of this section were used in the notifications. One interesting counter notification found was from netcopyrightlaw.com

This was, by far, one of the best counter notifications I have ever read.

The author referenced which area of title 17 applied, According to the counter notification, clarecountyinternet.com and serendipityinn.net filed copyright notifications to Google. According to the counter notification, Google responded around July 29, 2002 by removing information located at netcopyrightlaw.com from its files and caches, even information that was not relevant to the complaint. The person making the counter notification allegedly never received notification from Google regarding the receipt of a takedown of materials which had prior to the complaint appeared in search results at Google. Instead of showing the results for the website, the user received information relevant to a DMCA notification being filed and the search results being removed.

The amusing part of this tale is that netcopyrightlaw.com content includes information about copyright law cases. Netcopyright actually included in their good faith statement that they believed there was misrepresentation on the part of the people filing the copyright notification.

Today, you can find netcopyrightlaw in a Google search.

> Google is a search engine. They offer a service to users. Look at it like a restaurant. "We reserve the right to refuse service to anyone."

> One fascinating aspect of this is that a search engine's time is monopolized by so many notifications and counter notifications which ultimately is a cost in time and money when those funds could be put to better use for the company.

INFORMATION RESIDING ON SYSTEMS OR NETWORKS AT DIRECTION OF USERS

512 (c)(1)

IN GENERAL

A service provider shall not be liable for monetary relief, or, except as provided in subsection (j), for injunctive or other equitable relief, for infringement of copyright by reason of the storage at the direction of a user of material that resides on a system or network controlled or operated by or for the service provider, if the service provider

A. i. does not have actual knowledge that the material or an activity using the material on the system or network is infringing

ii. in the absence of such actual knowledge, is not aware of facts or circumstances from which infringing activity is apparent; or

iii. upon obtaining such knowledge or awareness, acts expeditiously to remove, or disable access to, the material

B. does not receive a financial benefit directly attributable to the infringing activity, in a case in which the service provider has the right and ability to control such activity; and

C. upon notification of claimed infringement as described in paragraph (3), responds expeditiously to remove, or disable access to, the material that is claimed to be infringing or to be the subject of infringing activity.

What is a DMCA agent?
DMCA Agents: 512 (c) (2)

Many companies have a DMCA agent. The DMCA agent handles the notifications, counter notifications and works to remedy any alleged infringement claims that are valid according to company policy and the law.

A complete list of DMCA agents is located at the Library of Congress Copyright site.

http://www.copyright.gov/onlinesp/list/

The Register of Copyrights maintains a directory of agents available to the public. Service providers may be subject to a fee for maintaining a current directory. Currently, the fee is 80 dollars.

GoDaddy is an ICANN accredited registrar and according to their website, the world's largest domain name registrar. This company is located in Scottsdale, AZ and I used to drive by this place each day on my way to my day job. I had no idea they had over 9 million domains to manage! The company was founded in 1997. By 2004, GoDaddy was ranked 8 on the 2004 Inc. 500 list of the nation's fastest-growing privately held companies.

GoDaddy receives DMCA notifications and according to their DMCA agent, a very nice gentleman, as long as the claims meet the requirements for a notification, the site is left down for 10 days. While there are some counter notifications, many people take down whatever content allegedly infringes copyright, because the domain owners would rather not have their sites left down for any period of time. Users understand through the agreement for service the terms of service.

Over the past five years, several calls to DMCA agents were made. In each case, the agent was very amicable and helpful. However, there seems to be difficulty in accessing empirical data relevant to actual numbers of DMCA notices. There are no set regulations as to determine how many notifications are received or how many counter notifications are received. Research in that area is limited to the resources available through Chilling Effects and word of mouth.

Notifications, Removal of Materials, Disabling Access, and Counter Notifications

Included in the DMCA are the guidelines for filing notifications, informing users, disabling access or removing materials, and counter notifications. Below is a flow chart that is representative of the process.

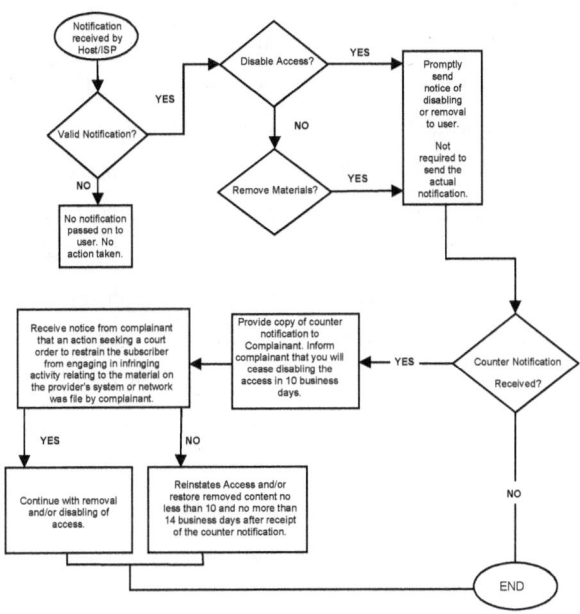

ELEMENTS of NOTIFICATION
Title 512 (c) (3)

The notification must be written and provided to the designated agent of the service provider and include:
A physical or electronic signature of the person authorized to act on behalf of the owner of an exclusive right that is allegedly infringed. This could be a lawyer, legal representative, copyright owner, etc.

- Identification of the copyrighted work. If there are multiple copyrighted works at one online site those that are to be covered by one notification, a list of the works must be included.
- Identification of the material that is allegedly infringing. This is the material that is intended to be removed or access to which is to be disabled.
- The information for identification must be "reasonably sufficient" for the service provider to locate the material most likely for the sole purpose of determining the content is present and for the removing or disabling of access to the materials allegedly infringing.
- The address, phone number and if available, the email address where the complainant can be contacted.
- A statement that the complaining party has a good faith belief that use of the material in the manner complained of is not

authorized by the copyright owner, its agent, or the law.

- A statement that the information in the notification is accurate, and under penalty of perjury, that the complaining party is authorized to act on behalf of the owner of an exclusive right that is allegedly infringed.

Some of the Cease and Desist notices reviewed, such as the one by the College Board to Fairtest, were not in compliance with this requirement.

Notifications that do not comply

Any notification from a copyright owner or person authorized to act on behalf of the copyright owner, does not comply "substantially" with the provisions of above will not be considered in determining whether a service provider has actual knowledge or is aware of facts or circumstances from which infringing activity is apparent. In other words, the notification that is not valid will not be considered a factor to determine the ISP had actual knowledge of alleged infringing activity.

When the notification to the DMCA agent complies with 2, 3, or 4 of the previous section but not the rest, the notification can be considered in determining if the provider had actual knowledge or is aware of alleged infringing activity. In order to maintain exemption from actual knowledge, the service provider must promptly attempt to contact the person making the notification or takes other reasonable steps to assist in the receipt of notification that substantially complies with all the provisions of elements of notification. The ISP could be found liable and considered to have actual knowledge if the invalid notification includes:

2. Identification of the copyrighted work. If there are multiple copyrighted works at one online site those that are to be covered by one notification, a list of the works must be included.

3. Identification of the material that is allegedly infringing. This is the material that is intended to be removed or access to which is

to be disabled.

4. The information for identification must be "reasonably sufficient" for the service provider to locate the material most likely for the sole purpose of determining the content is present and for the removing or disabling of access to the materials allegedly infringing.

The ISP could be found liable if the ISP does not attempt to contact the claimant or "take other reasonable steps" to assist in obtaining a notification that complies with the elements of notification – only if the original notification includes specific identification of the copyrighted work, identification of the material that is infringing, and that information is reasonably sufficient to locate the material. If there specific identification is not complete, the ISP need do nothing more.

In a case where the notification includes substantial information of identification of the copyrighted work, identification of the material that is allegedly infringing, and is reasonably sufficient to locate materials, the ISP may be considered to have knowledge and the ISP holds the responsibility to pursue the matter with the claimant in obtaining a notification that complies. This does not seem to state that the material or access be removed based on an invalid claim. Another, valid claim must be filed in order to take down the access.

INFORMATION LOCATION TOOLS
512 (d)

Summary

A service provider is not liable for referring or linking users to locations online containing infringing materials by using "information location tools".

• if the service provider doesn't have actual knowledge that the material or activity is infringing;

• in the absence of actual knowledge, is not aware of facts or circumstances from which infringing activity is apparent; or

• upon obtaining such knowledge or awareness, acts expeditiously to remove, or disable access to, the material;

• does not receive a financial gain directly attributable to the infringing activity, in a case in which the service provider has the right and ability to control such activity; and

• upon notification of claimed infringement responds "expeditiously" to remove, or disable access to, the material that is claimed to be infringing or to be the subject of infringing activity or a reference or link, to material that is claimed to be infringing, that is set to be removed or access disabled. The information must be sufficient for the service provider to locate the reference or link.

Definition

Information Location Tool

Including a directory, index, reference, pointer, or hypertext link.

According to the copyright office summary December 1998, this includes search engines.

http://www.copyright.gov/legislation/dmca.pdf

Consider the following:

1. This section includes responding to remove or disable access to materials claimed to be infringing or a reference to a link to the material that is claimed to be infringing that is set to be removed or access disabled. Is this limited to on the specific server or does this mean a link to another site or FTP?

2. With regards to linking, how does this affect a search engine?

LIMITATION ON LIABILITY OF NONPROFIT
EDUCATIONAL INSTITUTIONS
512 (e)

Summary

A public or nonprofit institution of higher education as a service provider:

When a faculty member or graduate student who is an employee of an institution, as described above, is performing the duties of teaching or a research function, the faculty member or graduate student shall be considered to be a person other than the institution. Knowledge or awareness of infringing activities by faculty members or graduate students are not be attributed to the institution, if:

- the infringing activities of the faculty member or graduate student do not involve
- providing online access to instructional materials that are or were required or recommended, over the past 3-year period, for a course taught at the institution by faculty member or graduate student;
- the institution has not, received more than two notifications of claimed infringement by faculty member or graduate student over the past 3 years, and such notifications of claimed infringement were not actionable under subsection (f); and
- the institution provides to all users of its system or network informational materials that accurately describe, and promote

compliance with, the laws of the United States relating to copyright.

"Injunctive relief relevant to j2 and j3 limitations apply."

The Technology, Education, and Copyright Harmonization Act of 2002 (TEACH) provides provisions related to online education and copyright.

MISREPRESENTATIONS
512 (f)

Summary

This section is fairly straightforward and covers misrepresentations from either side of the fence.

Misrepresentation includes anyone who knowingly misrepresents that :

1. material or activity is infringing
2. material or activity was removed or disabled by mistake or misidentification,

This section poses a threat to those who make notification claims and to those who make counter notifications. However, if the person believes they are well within their legal right to post, use or provide the content, the imposed damages should not apply.

Those who make the notification claim should be sure before they act on infringing materials. In the case of several larger corporations, they have made frivolous claims of infringement. One such claim regarded an mp3 of a Professor Usher. Another notification was received by archive.org with regard to a movie called U-571. While archive.org did have some movies with 571 in the link, these links did not go to the movie U-571, according to a letter by the digital librarian to UNIVERSAL STUDIOS, INC. Archive.org also maintains itself as an archive and according to the DMCA, archives have an exemption. Regardless, according to this notification, there was no movie U-571.

http://www.chillingeffects.org/responses/notice.cgi?NoticeID=597

Should the RIAA and Universal be liable for damages, including costs and attorneys' fees, incurred by the alleged infringer, who is injured by such misrepresentation, as the result of the service provider relying upon such misrepresentation in removing or disabling access to the material or activity claimed to be infringing, or in replacing the removed material or ceasing to disable access to it?

If there was injury, then that might constitute a good case and I encourage anyone who experiences such injury to consider this information.

Proving that the person filing the complaint knowingly misrepresented could be challenging. However, to be reasonable, any complaint should be thoroughly investigated before a notification is filed. Frivolous notifications based on filenames and extensions would seem unacceptable and at the very least, unethical, in practice.

REPLACEMENT OF REMOVED OR DISABLED MATERIAL AND LIMITATION ON OTHER LIABILITY: Title 512 (g)

Summary

A service provider is not liable to any person for any claim based on the service provider's good faith disabling of access to, or removal of, material or activity claimed to be infringing or based on facts or circumstances from which infringing activity is apparent, regardless of whether the material or activity is ultimately determined to be infringing.

This does not apply to material that is removed or where access is disabled by the service provider based on a DMCA notification unless the following conditions are met:

- The provider must take reasonable steps promptly to notify the subscriber or user that they have removed or disabled access to the material.

- If a counter-notification is received, the provider must inform the person filing the complaint that the materials that were removed, will be replaced within 10 business days. In a case where access was disabled, the provider will inform the complainant that the service provider will cease disabling the access in 10 business days.

- The provider will replace the removed material and ceases disabling access to it not less than 10, nor more than 14, business days following receipt of the counter notice unless the complainant notifies the service provider that a court action "seeking a court order to restrain the subscriber from engaging in infringing activity relating to the material on the service provider's system or network" is filed.

What this basically means is that someone can come along and file a DMCA notification against you. You file a counter notification because the claim is unsubstantiated or worse, misrepresentation. The site will not be up in the previous condition until at least 10 days. If the site is not back up or the access is not enabled within 14 days, the ISP is liable.

That is, of course, unless the person filing the notification seeks a court order to restrain you from "engaging in infringing activity related to the materials" on the provider's network. The GoDaddy DMCA agent confirms that they are required by law to keep the site down for 10 days.

See Wendy Seltzer and the NFL for some additional information regarding receipt of a notification for material that was previously removed and then restored.

What do I do if I get a DMCA notification?

If you receive a DMCA notice alleging infringement from a copyright author or owner, read it. If you believe the claim to be legitimate and within the scope of the law, take whatever provisions you think or feel necessary. In some cases, seeking legal advice is recommended. In other cases, alleged infringement or copyright violation is a scare tactic used by others to threaten, impeach speech and stop competition.

What is a counter notification?
Contents of Counter Notifications
512 (g) (3)

Summary

A counter notification is written statement by the person who has access restricted or materials removed by an ISP or host due to a DMCA copyright infringement claim and notification by a copyright owner or representative of a copyright owner.
The counter notification is sent to the ISP. This is written communication to the ISP Customer relations, DMCA agent or representative responsible for handling DMCA complaints and counter notifications.

The ISP is then required to resume service within 10 to 14 business days unless Complainant provides notification that they has filed paperwork seeking a restraining order.

How do you file a counter notification?

To file a counter notification:
provide in writing by fax or snail mail

Your name, phone number, email address.

If applicable, the specific material alleged as infringing that was removed with location.

If applicable, the specific alleged reason for disabled access.

A statement that you, (or)the Respondent, consents to the jurisdiction of Federal District Court for the judicial district in which Respondent's address is located (or Delaware County, if Respondent's address is outside of the United States), and that Respondent will accept service of process originating from Complainant or an agent of Complainant.

"I swear, under penalty of perjury, that I have a good faith belief that each image or article identified above was removed or disabled as a result of a mistake or misidentification of the material to be removed or disabled."

Signature of the Respondent or a representative person authorized to act on behalf of Respondent.

Sample Counter Notification

Date

ISP (or provider)

ISP Address

DMCA Agent Name, where applicable

To Whom It May Concern,

This is a counter-notification as authorized in § 512(g) of the U.S. Copyright Law. In good faith, the material that was removed or disabled as a result of the Notice of Infringement was a result of mistake or misidentification of the material. I respectfully request that access be enabled and any removed content, be replaced to the following:

[Identify the content that was removed or where access was disabled.]

[Identify the location where the content appeared before it was removed or access disabled.]

My contact information is as follows:

[Your name, address, telephone number, and email].

I consent to the jurisdiction of Federal District Court for the judicial district in which the address is located and I agree to accept service of process from the person who provided notification under subsection (c)(1)(C) or an agent thereof.

[if your address is outside of the United States: I consent for any judicial district in which the service provider may be

found, and that the I will accept service of process from the person who provided notification under subsection (c)(1)(C) or an agent of such person.]

I have a good faith belief that the material removed or disabled following the Notice of Infringement was removed or disabled because of mistake or misidentification of the material. I therefore request that the material be replaced and/or no longer disabled.
I declare under the perjury laws of the United States of America that this notification is true and correct.

Signature (either electronic or physical)
Name

SUBPOENAS TO IDENTIFY INFRINGER:
Title 512 (h)

REQUEST

The copyright owner or representative can request the clerk of any US court to issue a subpoena to a Service Provider for the identity of an alleged infringer as long as it follows these guidelines when filing with the clerk:

- a copy of a notification
- a proposed subpoena
- a sworn declaration regarding the purpose of the subpoena is to get the identity of the alleged infringer and will only be used for the purposes of protecting rights under the DMCA – copyright violation.

CONTENTS OF SUBPOENA

The subpoena will authorize and order the service provider that is the recipient of the notification to disclose to the copyright owner, the identity of the alleged infringer relevant to the notification filed, granted the service provider has that information relevant to the alleged infringer.

BASIS FOR GRANTING SUBPOENA

If a valid notification is filed and the proposed subpoena is in proper order, along with a declaration from the copyright owner or representative, the clerk will issue and sign the subpoena and give it to the copyright owner or representative to deliver to the service provider.

ACTIONS OF SERVICE PROVIDER RECEIVING SUBPOENA

When the service provider gets the subpoena, the provider must quickly act in giving information to the copyright owner or representative required by the subpoena.

RULES APPLICABLE TO SUBPOENA

The procedure for issuance and delivery of the subpoena, and the remedies for noncompliance with the subpoena, are governed by the Federal Rules of Civil Procedure governing the issuance, service, and enforcement of a subpoena duces tecum.

The Subpoena Rule, Rule 45, according to www.supremecourtus.gov/orders/courtorders/frcv05p.pdf

According to Bill Summary & Status for the 108th Congress, the Latest Major Action took place on 9/16/2003 and this bill was referred to Senate committee. "Status: Read twice and referred to the Committee on Commerce, Science, and Transportation."
More information about the Charter Communications and Verizon case is found in this book.

TITLE III

COMPUTER MAINTENANCE OR REPAIR COPYRIGHT EXEMPTION

SHORT TITLE
Section 301

Summary

Title III contains provisions for computer maintenance and repair.

Legal Reference: DMCA > TITLE III > Section 301
SEC. 301. SHORT TITLE.

This title may be cited as the `Computer Maintenance Competition Assurance Act'.

LIMITATIONS ON EXCLUSIVE RIGHTS; COMPUTER PROGRAMS
Section 302

Summary

For the purposes of maintaining or repairing a computer, a user can make or authorize the making of a copy of applications as long as it is made entirely for the purpose of activation of a machine that legally contains an authorized copy for reasons of maintenance and repair. The copy is not to be used in any other way and this section requires the legally created copy be destroyed immediately after maintenance or repair is completed.

Title IV

TITLE IV--MISCELLANEOUS PROVISIONS

PROVISIONS RELATING TO THE COMMISSIONER OF PATENTS AND TRADEMARKS AND THE REGISTER OF COPYRIGHTS

Sec. 401

Summary

This section includes some of the duties and functions of the Register of Copyrights.

These duties included in this section are:

1. Advise Congress on national and international issues relating to copyright, other matters arising under this title, and related matters.

2. Provide information and assistance to Federal departments and agencies and the Judiciary on national and international issues relating to copyright, other matters arising under this title, and related matters.

3. Participate in meetings of international intergovernmental organizations and meetings with foreign government officials relating to copyright, other matters arising under this title, and related matters, including as a member of United States delegations as authorized by the appropriate Executive branch authority.

4. Conduct studies and programs regarding copyright, other matters arising under this title, and related matters, the

administration of the Copyright Office, or any function vested in the Copyright Office by law, including educational programs conducted cooperatively with foreign intellectual property offices and international intergovernmental organizations.

5. Perform such other functions as Congress may direct, or as may be appropriate in furtherance of the functions and duties specifically set forth in this title.

EPHEMERAL RECORDINGS

Sec. 402

Summary

This section offers broadcasters similar rights offered in analog broadcast to a digital environment. Circumvention of technological measures of protection could be possible under certain circumstances.

LIMITATIONS ON EXCLUSIVE RIGHTS; DISTANCE EDUCATION.

RECOMMENDATIONS BY REGISTER OF COPYRIGHTS

Sec. 403 (a)

Within 6 months of enactment, the Register of Copyrights will get consultation from copyright owners, nonprofit educational institutions and nonprofit libraries/archives and submit a recommendation to Congress on promoting distance education and using digital technologies.

This was to include

Interactive networks while maintaining a balance in the rights of owners and users.

FACTORS

Sec. 403 (b)

The Register of copyrights should consider:

1. the need for an exemption from exclusive rights of copyright owners for distance education through digital networks

2. the categories of works to be included under any distance education exemption

3. the extent of appropriate quantitative limitations on the portions of works that may be used under any distance education exemption

4. the parties who should be entitled to the benefits of any distance education exemption

5. the parties who should be designated as eligible recipients of distance education materials under any distance education exemption

6. whether and what types of technological measures can or should be employed to safeguard against unauthorized access to, and use or retention of, copyrighted materials as a condition of eligibility for any distance education exemption, including, in light of developing technological capabilities, the exemption set out in section 110(2) of title 17, United States Code

7. the extent to which the availability of licenses for the use of copyrighted works in distance education through interactive digital networks should be considered in assessing eligibility for any distance education exemption; and

8. such other issues relating to distance education through interactive digital networks that the Register considers appropriate.

In 2002, the Technology, Education, and Copyright Harmonization Act was passed. This act included information regarding distance education and copyright.

EXEMPTION FOR LIBRARIES AND ARCHIVES.

Sec. 404

Summary

This section allows for the preservation of information by libraries and archives. With the change in medium, access to the materials was impossible unless an obsolete medium was used. Therefore, this section allows libraries and archives to preserve this information in a digital manner.

The following are factors to take into consideration for this exemption:

➢ If the existing format is obsolete, and if after a "reasonable effort" fails in locating a replacement at a fair price,

➢ If the item is not available legally to the public in a format outside the premises of the library or archive

➢ If the format is considered obsolete if the machine or device necessary is no longer manufactured or reasonably available in the commercial marketplace.

SCOPE OF EXCLUSIVE RIGHTS IN SOUND RECORDINGS; EPHEMERAL RECORDINGS

Sec. 405

This section allowed webcasters to be considered subscription transmissions. This allowed webcasters to transmit but came with a possible usage fee.

ASSUMPTION OF CONTRACTUAL OBLIGATIONS RELATED TO TRANSFERS OF RIGHTS IN MOTION PICTURES

Sec. 406

This section is related to the transfer of copyright ownership with regards to motion pictures.

TITLE V. PROTECTION OF CERTAIN ORIGINAL DESIGNS

TITLE V – SEC. 501 and 502

These sections are the short title and technical amendments

Chapter 13 – Hull Vessel Design

Chapter 13 covers the protection of original designs. This section is relevant to the protection of boat hull designs. Title V is included in the DMCA due to concerns by boat manufacturers and design firms based on the decision in Bonito Boats Inc. v. ThunderCraft Boats Inc.

Bonito Boats Inc. v. ThunderCraft Boats Inc. Case

The court stated that "efficient operation of the federal patent system depends upon substantially free trade in publicly known, unpatented design and utilitarian conceptions."

17 USCS 102(b) provides that in no case does copyright protection for an original work of authorship extend to any idea, procedure, process, system, method of operation, concept, principle, or discovery.

The design of boat hulls was protected from copying by making a mold of the final hull in the state of Florida, but the Supreme Court decided to strike down this protection in the decision. Effectively, the Supreme Court's decision would not allow patent like protection at the state level.

Boat designers must apply for registration within 2 years of the time the design is publicized. The registered owner would hold the rights to sell, import, distribute for commercial use.

The DMCA protects educational endeavors with regard to these designs. Anyone distributing the vessel hull that was protected is not liable if they do not know the design was protected. Any publicly distributed hull must have a notification that the design is protected. If there is no notice, the owner can not file a claim for damages.

Information regarding this case can be found in many places online including:

http://www.law.uconn.edu/homes/swilf/ip/cases/bonito.htm

EXEMPTIONS ADDED

Exemptions

The following are approved exemptions. These exemptions were specifically related to section 1201 – prohibition on circumvention of technological measures that control access to copyrighted works. The process includes comments, hearings, and rulemaking. The term of the exempted classes is 3 years.

These are the exemptions listed on the Library of Congress website at: http://www.copyright.gov/1201/

2000

1. Compilations consisting of lists of websites blocked by filtering software applications; and

2. Literary works, including computer programs and databases, protected by access control mechanisms that fail to permit access because of malfunction, damage, or obsoleteness.

2003

1. Compilations consisting of lists of Internet locations blocked by commercially marketed filtering software applications that are intended to prevent access to domains, websites or portions of websites, but not including lists of Internet locations blocked by software applications that operate exclusively to protect against damage to a computer or computer network or lists of Internet locations blocked by software applications that operate exclusively to prevent receipt of email.

2. Computer programs protected by dongles that prevent access due to malfunction or damage and which are obsolete.

3. Computer programs and video games distributed in formats that have become obsolete and which require the original media or hardware as a condition of access.

4. Literary works distributed in ebook format when all existing ebook editions of the work (including digital text editions made available by authorized entities) contain access controls that prevent the enabling of the ebook's read-aloud function and that prevent the enabling of screen readers to render the text into a specialized format.

http://www.copyright.gov/1201/docs/librarian_statement_01.html

2006

Persons making non infringing uses of the following six classes of works will not be subject to the prohibition against circumventing access controls (17 U.S.C. § 1201(a)(1)) during the next three years.

1. Audiovisual works included in the educational library of a college or university's film or media studies department, when circumvention is accomplished for the purpose of making compilations of portions of those works for educational use in the classroom by media studies or film professors.

2. Computer programs and video games distributed in formats that have become obsolete and that require the original media or hardware as a condition of access, when circumvention is accomplished for the purpose of preservation or archival reproduction of published digital works by a library or archive. A format shall be considered obsolete if the machine or system necessary to render perceptible a work stored in that format is no longer manufactured or is no longer reasonably available in the commercial marketplace.

3. Computer programs protected by dongles that prevent access due to malfunction or damage and which are obsolete. A dongle shall be considered obsolete if it is no longer manufactured or if a replacement or repair is no longer reasonably available in the commercial marketplace.

4. Literary works distributed in ebook format when all existing ebook editions of the work (including digital text editions made available by authorized entities) contain access controls that prevent the enabling either of the book's read-aloud function or of screen readers that render the text into a specialized format.

5. Computer programs in the form of firmware that enable wireless telephone handsets to connect to a wireless telephone communication network, when circumvention is accomplished for the sole purpose of lawfully connecting to a wireless telephone communication network.

6. Sound recordings, and audiovisual works associated with those sound recordings, distributed in compact disc format and protected by technological protection measures that control access to lawfully purchased works and create or exploit security flaws or vulnerabilities that compromise the security of personal computers, when circumvention is accomplished solely for the purpose of good faith testing,

investigating, or correcting such security flaws or vulnerabilities.

2009

The final rulemaking order will be issued in October 2009.

www.ingramcontent.com/pod-product-compliance
Lightning Source LLC
Chambersburg PA
CBHW070049210526
45170CB00012B/622